"...in all patriotic enterprises the services of one woman are equal to those of seven men and a half." - Dr. Clarke in Lossing's *Field-Book of the Revolution,* 1859

Molly Pitcher, cover, left us no portrait, so our publisher, Ellen Knill, posed for the artist, Lt. Col. Donna Neary, USMC.

HANNAH WHITE ARNETT

In the summer of 1776, Americans fighting for independence began to feel battered and despairing. Two British brothers, Admiral Richard Howe and General William Howe, had defeated colonists at Long Island, White Plains, Fort Washington and Fort Lee.

To crush the American uprising once and for all, the Howes issued a proclamation in November 1776. They would pardon all colonists who would declare their allegiance to Great Britain within sixty days, they said.

The offer sounded especially tempting in New Jersey, where redcoats were in fast pursuit of General Washington's half-starved and half-clothed troops. In Elizabethtown, a group of colonists met to discuss the offer in the home of Isaac Arnett. They debated long into the night, and finally decided that the American cause was hopeless. The smartest course of action, they agreed, was to accept the British offer.

At this point, Isaac's wife, Hannah, appeared in the doorway. She had heard the discussion from an adjoining room, and she was furious.

"Have you chosen the part of men or traitors?" she demanded. "You have forgotten one thing which England has not and which we have--one thing which outweighs all England's treasure--and that is the right. God is on our side, and every volley of our muskets is an echo of his voice. We are poor, weak, and few, but God is fighting for us. We entered into this struggle with pure hearts and prayerful lips. We had counted the cost and were willing to pay the price, were it in our hearts' blood. And now, now because for a time the day is going against us, you would give up all and sneak back like cravens to kiss the feet that have trampled upon us. And you call yourselves men! The sons of those who gave up home and fortune and fatherland to make for themselves and for dear liberty a resting place in the wilderness! Oh shame upon you, cowards!"

Hannah went on and on. In tears, she ended her speech by threatening to leave her home and husband unless the men changed their minds. When the meeting ended, each man had pledged his support to the cause of freedom.

Many timid men were encouraged to join the fight for freedom by their patriotic wives or sweethearts.

Hannah White Arnett

ANNE BAILEY

When Indians tortured her husband to death at the Battle of Point Pleasure in 1774, Anne Bailey wanted to help make the frontier safe for others. She left her seven-year-old son with a neighbor, took a long rifle and began riding alone throughout Indian territory in the Kanawha Valley of Virginia. A full-blown American revolution was about to break out against the British, and the countryside was full of warring Indians. Anne rode from settlement to settlement recruiting colonists to serve in the militia.

Anne's wilderness survival skills were as sharp as any Indian's, and once the war began, she made good use of them by serving as a scout and messenger.

Anne rode fearlessly through enemy territory to deliver vital information to distant outposts. At night she slept in caves and hollow trees to keep her ammunition dry, and she was always careful not to be discovered by Indians who might be tracking her. Before Anne settled down for the night, she would ride a half mile past her campsite, then turn her horse loose and walk back to the place to sleep in safety.

Anne Bailey clad in homespun dress and armed with an American long rifle.

One winter night, wind and snow made it impossible for Anne to build a fire and keep warm. She crawled into a hollow tree and held her horse's head close so that the animal's warm breath would keep her from freezing.

Another time Anne was being followed by hostile Indians, so she crawled into a hollow log. The Indians searched all around the area, and even sat on top of the log Anne was hiding in. Anne remained hidden while the Indians rode away with her favorite horse, Liverpool.

That night after dark, she tracked the Indians to their camp. Moving silently through the woods, Anne spotted Liverpool among the other horses. Then, with a terrifying, rebellious scream, she leaped onto Liverpool's back and galloped off to safety.

Colonists who weren't so daring began calling her "Mad Anne." She became famous among the Indians as the "White Squaw of Kanawha."

After Americans won their independence, Anne served heroically as a scout in the battle against Indians on the western Virginia frontier.

Anne Bailey

PENELOPE PAGETT BARKER

It was October 1774, nearly a year after a group of men disguised as Mohawk Indians dumped chests of imported tea into Boston Harbor to protest British taxes. North Carolina's First Provincial Congress had banned East India tea and manufactured goods imported from England, but the foreign tea and cloth were still available throughout the state.

Now a group of fifty-one women in Edenton, North Carolina were preparing to take on the British Parliament. Penelope Barker had organized the gathering of wives, daughters and sisters of some of the leading citizens of Edenton. She had composed a resolution declaring that they would no longer drink tea from Britain or use cloth manufactured there. Penelope presented her resolution, and the women discussed it. Some of them had relatives living in England, and Edenton's economy was tied heavily to its commerce with the West Indies. Furthermore, giving up tea was a real hardship for the colonists, and the tea tax was not particularly heavy; most colonists merely resented paying it without having representation in Britain's Parliament.

A lady of Edenton, North Carolina toasts the patriotic cause with a cup of tea brewed from dried raspberry leaves.

But all fifty-one women signed the resolution that day, and then chatted over cups of tea brewed from dried raspberry leaves. By pledging not to drink British tea themselves, the women automatically included all the other members of their households. In the coming weeks, the women would carefully watch one another to make sure no one was shirking her patriotic duty by purchasing British goods.

When news of the "Edenton Tea Party" reached England, the reaction was swift and strong. A London newspaper published a cartoon making fun of the Edenton women. One Londoner sarcastically wrote that the women of Edenton might "crush us into atoms by their omnipotency; the only security on our side to prevent the impending ruin, that I can perceive, is the probability that there are but few places in America which possess so much female artillery as Edenton."

But there was no mistaking the significance of Penelope Barker's resolution. It proved that women in the colonies were resisting "Mother Country" England; and unlike the men who hid their identities at the Boston Tea Party, the women of Edenton had signed their names in open defiance of the British.

Penelope Pagett Barker

MARGARET COCHRAN CORBIN

General George Washington allowed a number of soldiers' wives to travel with each company in the Continental army. Twenty-five-year-old Molly Corbin was married to John Corbin, a gunner, an artillery man who loaded and fired cannons for the First Company of the Pennsylvania Artillery. Molly was among those wives who cooked for the men, washed and mended clothes and nursed the sick and wounded. Though the work was abundant and hard, Molly sometimes watched John's daily drills and learned the gunnery routine.

In mid-November 1776, when John and Molly were stationed in Fort Washington, New York, nearly9,000 British and Hessian soldiers were bombarding the fort. Only 2,800 Americans were there to face the attack from warships in the river below.

Molly refused to leave her husband's side in his two-gun battery as shells fell around them. When the gunner in charge fell dead, John quickly took over and Molly became his assistant. Together they kept the cannon roaring down at the enemy. Then, in a sudden loud explosion, Molly saw her husband reel back from the cannon. A direct hit had killed him.

Though distraught with grief and shock, Molly knew what she must do. She took the ramrod and stepped to John's place with the cannon. As the battle raged until late that afternoon, she continued loading and firing the cannon until she, too, felt hot British grapeshot tear through her shoulder. A shower of small iron balls had lacerated her jaw, mangled her chest and nearly tore her left arm from her body. Soldiers carried Molly to the rear, where she received first aid.

When the fighting stopped, the British and Hessians had captured Fort Washington, and the American survivors became their prisoners. The British put the American wounded on parole and Molly, together with the wounded men, was ferried across the river to Fort Lee. From there she was taken nearly one hundred miles in a jolting wagon to Philadelphia.

Molly never fully recovered from her wounds, and in April 1783, was mustered out of service. She became the first woman ever to receive a lifetime pension from the United States government and spent the rest of her days near West Point, New York, where she was known as "Captain Molly."

Margaret Corbin was strong and brave enough to handle the heavy, dirty, dangerous task of serving a muzzle-loading cannon.

Margaret Corbin

LYDIA BARRINGTON DARRAGH

The British occupied Philadelphia, Pennsylvania, from September 1777 to June 1778, and Lydia Barrington Darragh lived almost directly across the street from the headquarters of British general William Howe. One of Howe's officers was Lydia's cousin, and he arranged to use a large room on the second floor of the Darragh house for British staff meetings.

One night in early December, after the Darragh family had gone to bed, the British officers planned a secret attack on the American army encamped sixteen miles away at White Marsh. As they plotted, Lydia quietly snuck out of her room and crouched on the floor outside the meeting room to listen. In two days, the British would march 5,000 soldiers to surprise Washington's troops. If successful, they might capture the entire American army.

Lydia Darragh walks through the snow to White Marsh to warn the American soldiers.

When Lydia had heard the details, she crept back to her room and lay in bed worrying. General Washington must be warned, she thought. Her twenty-two-year-old son was serving with the Continental army at White Marsh!

The next morning, Lydia told her husband that the family needed flour, and she set off for Pearson's Mill in Frankford, five miles away. When she arrived at the mill, Lydia left her flour sack and continued walking north through light snow toward Whitemarsh. Before she finished the long trek through uninhabited territory, she met an American officer on horseback. She told him of the British plan, and then returned home, stopping at the mill to pick up a sack of flour.

Lydia knew she would be hanged if the British discovered what she had done, and she was nervous. She couldn't sleep the following night, so she watched from a window as the British marched out of town toward White Marsh.

A few days later, a British officer knocked at Lydia's door. He ordered her into the meeting room, and demanded to know if all the Darraghs had been in bed on the night the White Marsh attack was planned. She assured him that they were. The officer went on to explain that "We were betrayed, for, on arriving near the encampment of General Washington, we found his cannon mounted, his troops under arms and so prepared at every point to receive us that we were compelled to march back, without injuring our enemy, like a parcel of fools."

Lydia Barrington Darragh

DEBORAH SAMPSON GANNETT

The colonists' war for independence was dragging on, and twenty-one-year-old Deborah Sampson knew that General Washington's soldiers were having a hard time. The restless and adventuresome young woman longed to do something to help the revolution, so she hatched an unusual plan.

On a spring night in 1781, Deborah stole away from her farm home in Middleborough, Massachusetts. She walked to nearby woods and changed into a man's suit that she had secretly sewn from coarse cloth. Deborah continued walking northward for about thirty miles to Bellingham. There she enlisted in the Fourth Massachusetts regiment of the Continental army as "Robert Shurtleff." On May 23 she was mustered into service at Worcester.

Deborah Sampson Gannet in the uniform of the Light Company of the 4th Massachusetts. Coat with white facings, white small clothes, red tip on plume.

Deborah was physically strong, and at five feet, seven inches, she was taller than most women. She hid her feminine figure by tightly binding her breasts, and though the men in her company teased her about not having to shave, they assumed that "the blooming boy" was simply too young to grow a beard. After all, Deborah drilled, marched and performed a soldier's duties as well as the men who served with her.

Deborah's regiment was sent to West Point River, where she was assigned to a company of light cavalry. She went on scouting and raiding expeditions, and in one clash with British dragoons, was shot once through the coat and once through the cap. In another skirmish, she was slashed by a saber, a wound that she insisted on treating herself.

When Deborah was wounded in a small engagement at Tarrytown, New York, she feared that her secret was in danger. A bullet had lodged in her left thigh, just below the groin, and though she begged her comrades not to take her to the camp hospital, they did anyway. When the surgeon arrived, Deborah showed him only a slight wound on her head. Later, when Deborah was all alone, she used a penknife to probe for the bullet in her thigh. She was unable to remove it, and it remained there the rest of her life.

But Deborah couldn't keep her secret forever. While serving as an orderly in Philadelphia, she contracted a fever, became delirious and was hospitalized. There the examining doctor placed his hand above Deborah's heart, found the tight bandage and discovered his patient was a woman. The doctor quietly made the necessary arrangements that ended her military career. Private Robert Shurtleff was honorably discharged from the United States Army by General Henry Knox at West Point on October 23, 1783. She had been the first woman to enlist as an American soldier.

Deborah Sampson Gannet

EMILY GEIGER

American general Nathanael Greene thought that if he and General Thomas Sumter combined forces, they could capture Fort Ninety-Six, South Carolina, from the British. But fifty miles of wild country and many British scouts stood between the two generals, and anyone caught carrying a message between them would be hanged.

Somehow eighteen-year old Emily Geiger, the daughter of a well-to-do patriot farmer, heard of the dilemma and volunteered to deliver the messsage. At first General Greene refused to let a young woman go on such a dangerous errand. But Emily argued that she knew the country well and that British scouts would be less suspicious of a girl messenger.

At last General Greene consented. He wrote a note of instructions to General Sumter and had Emily memorize it, word by word. In case of capture, he told her, she must destroy the note before the enemy saw it and try to deliver the message verbally to General Sumter.

Emily Geiger rides through wild country evading British scouts to deliver General Nathanael Greene's message to General Thomas Sumter.

Emily memorized the note and set out on the risky mission on horseback. To throw any enemy scout off track, she first traveled in the opposite direction from Sumter's camp. Then she detoured and headed the right way. Whenever she heard mounted men approach, she left the main road and traveled through woods. That night Emily stayed with a farm family who she knew was sympathetic to the American cause.

The next day Emily was riding away from the road in a dry swamp when, suddenly, a band of enemy scouts appeared and stopped her. Taken completely by surprise, Emily could not think of an innocent explanation for her presence there, and the soldiers became suspicious. They led her to a nearby farmhouse and asked the Tory farmer's wife to search the girl. Left alone in a bedroom, Emily tore General Greene's note into small pieces that she chewed and swallowed. The paper was so dry that it almost choked her, but she managed to eat it all. When the farmer's wife entered the room and made a thorough search, there was no sign of any message. The soldiers then apologized and even helped Emily back on her horse.

Going on by indirect routes, Emily at last reached General Sumter's camp, where she recited the message by memory to the grateful general. "South Carolina will never forget the debt of gratitude she owes to Emily Geiger," he told her.

Emily Geiger

NANCY MORGAN HART

Nancy Hart was six feet tall with sandy hair, a freckled face and crossed eyes. She lived in Georgia with her husband Benjamin and daughter Sukey. Nancy drank, swore and readily shot her gun--especially at Tories. She once shot a young Tory prankster in the shoulder for startling her horse. Another time she flung a ladle of boiling soup at a Tory.

Nancy worked hard for American freedom. She regularly crossed the Savannah River on a log raft to get information from an enemy camp in South Carolina and bring it back to the Georgia militia. Once she entered a British camp wearing men's clothing. Another time, when she met a lone Tory on the road, she took his musket and marched him to a patriot fort, where she turned him over to the commander.

The Tory raiders met their match when they encountered the fearless Nancy Hart.

One day Nancy was doing housework when a band of Tories stopped by and ordered her to prepare a meal for them. Other Tories had already stolen all of Nancy's pigs and cows, so the men demanded that Nancy cook the family's last turkey. Then they stacked their guns against the cabin wall and sat down at the table to drink some liquor. They heard Nancy send Sukey to the spring for water but did not know that the family hid a conch shell in a tree stump there for emergencies. By blowing into the conch, Sukey signaled Benjamin and some patriot neighbors, who were working nearby, to hurry to the Hart cabin.

Meanwhile, as the Tories were busy drinking and laughing, Nancy secretly pulled out several wedges of pine wood that were used to fill spaces between the logs of the cabin wall. Then she quietly slipped one gun after the other outside through the hole between the logs.

Suddenly, one of the Tories noticed that only two guns were left in the cabin. As he lunged forward, Nancy picked up a musket and pointed it at him. "I'll blow the head off the first man that rises!" she said. Because of Nancy's crossed eyes, every one of the Tories thought she was aiming at him. One man moved, and she shot him dead. Another started to get up, and she shot him too. When Benjamin arrived with the neighbors, he found one man dead, one wounded, and Nancy standing in the doorway, pointing the gun at her prisoners.

Now what? Shooting was too kind for the Tories, Nancy declared. So the group took their captives behind the cabin and hung them from a tree.

Nancy Hart

HANNAH HUNTER HENDEE

When Indian raiders under British command attacked Royalton, Vermont, one mid-October morning in 1780, Robert Hendee rushed off to alert American soldiers at nearby Bethel Fort. Before he left home, he instructed his twenty-seven-year-old wife, Hannah, to take their two children to the safety of the nearest neighbor's house. "Travel on the trail through the woods," he told her, "because the open road might be dangerous."

Hannah and the children set out through the woods, but were soon accosted by a scouting party of Indians. The Indians whisked seven-year-old Michael away from Hannah, intending to force him to become a soldier. The captors then disappeared into the woods with their prize.

Hannah was determined to rescue her son. She and daughter Lucretia hurried along the bank of the White River until they came opposite a British encampment where Hannah expected to find the kidnappers. An Indian, who assumed the young mother and daughter wanted to surrender, carried them across the one hundred yards of strong, deep river currents to the camp's British lieutenant.

In camp, Hannah begged the lieutenant to order the release of her son. At first he refused to have anything to do with the matter, but Hannah persisted. The lieutenant eventually issued the order, and after a heated argument, the angry Indians returned Michael to his mother.

As Hannah prepared to leave camp with both of her children, she saw several other little boys brought in by Indians. She demanded their release too, and the lieutenant issued a second order to the Indian captors, who were now furious. They stared at the small group of frightened boys huddled around Hannah. One waved a knife and grabbed Michael, who was holding tightly to his mother's hand. As the Indian jerked Michael, Hannah decided that if she didn't loosen her grip on her son, they all would be killed. For the second time, Michael had been stolen from her.

Again Hannah confronted the British lieutenant, who, again, ordered Michael released. When Hannah finally left camp, nine terrified children clung to her and to each other. The little group formed a chain to cross the river toward home.

Hannah Hendee

JEMIMA JOHNSON

When her husband returned to military duty in Virginia in 1777, Jemima Johnson was left behind with her children and other settlers in Bryan's Station, a frontier stockade near Lexington, Kentucky.

On a hot mid-August day in 1782, Jemima and the other stockade residents discovered that 600 Native American, British and Canadian soldiers were lurking in nearby woods and planning an attack. The men in the stockade prepared to defend the fort, but they knew they had a critical problem. The stockade had run out of water. They needed water, not only to drink, but to put out fires that the Indians would surely set with their flaming arrows.

During Indian attacks, women often loaded muskets and rifles for the men. Of course, many women fired them as well!

The usual practice in the stockade was for the women to go out the gate each morning and bring back the day's supply of water from a nearby spring. But anyone attempting to go out of the gate on that day might be shot.

Jemima presented a daring plan to the others. The enemy was counting on a surprise attack, she said. If the women did not go out for water as usual, the attackers would suspect the settlers had discovered their presence. But if the women walked boldly to the spring and brought back water as usual, maybe the attackers would be fooled into thinking their secret was safe. To keep the advantage of surprise, Jemima reasoned, they might let the women pass.

Jemima told the other women and girls that if they would promise to follow, she and her daughter, Betsy, would lead the group to the spring. After a brief discussion, the others agreed that the plan at least offered a chance of survival. They knew that without water, there was none.

So Jemima led the group of twelve women and sixteen girls out of the stockade. Although badly frightened, the group did its best to appear relaxed and unaware of what lay beyond the trees and bushes. Meanwhile, the men anxiously watched them from the stockade, their rifles ready.

When the women returned safely with their buckets and tubs filled with water and the gate had shut behind them, the Indians and Tories began their attack. The fight lasted two days and a night before the enemy, hearing that help was coming from Lexington, finally retreated.

Jemima Johnson

DICEY LANGSTON

Dicey Langston of South Carolina and her father were avid patriots, but they lived among Tories. While her brothers were away fighting with the Continental army, sixteen-year-old Dicey overheard the plans of the Bloody Scouts, a ruthless Tory gang. Before long, they figured out that she was carrying their secrets to her brother, who was in charge of a nearby patriot camp. The Bloody Scouts warned Dicey's father that her spying must stop, and the fearful Mr. Langston forbid Dicey to go to her brother's camp again. Dicey agreed, but that was before she learned that the Bloody Scouts planned to attack it.

Dicey Langston wades into a rain swollen river.

Without a word to her father, Dicey quietly slipped out of the house that night and made her way across marshes, streams and through dark woods. She came to a river that was swollen with the spring rains and bravely waded in. At midstream the water came up to her neck, and Dicey slipped in the swirling current. Nearly drowning, she regained her balance but lost her sense of direction. Luckily she continued the right way and trudged on to her brother's camp. When she arrived, Dicey was dripping wet and shivering from the cold, but she delivered the news to her brother: the Bloody Scouts would attack at dawn.

It was especially bad news for the Americans. They had just returned from an expedition and were hungry and exhausted. Dicey hastily built a fire and made hoecakes for the men, who stuffed them into their shot bags to eat on their flight from the camp. She then hurried back home and snuck wearily into bed just before dawn. She managed to appear at breakfast as usual so no one would suspect she had been out all night.

But when the Bloody Scouts failed to find the patriot soldiers in their camp that morning, they were certain Dicey had delivered a warning. They stormed into the Langston house, bent on revenge. When the leader pointed a gun at Mr. Langston, Dicey rushed between them to protect her father. The Tory gang finally left without harming either of them.

Another time, a Tory captain stopped Dicey on the road and threatened to kill her if she didn't give him the information he wanted. Dicey pulled open her riding habit and answered, "Shoot me if you dare. I will not tell you!" The captain was about to shoot when a companion knocked his gun upward, and Dicey escaped.

Dicey Langston

SYBIL LUDINGTON

HUZZAH! for Sybil Ludington!

Sixteen-year-old Sybil Ludington was helping to put her seven little brothers and sisters to bed one night in April 1777, when a rider galloped up to the family's home and gristmill in Fredericksburg, New York. The British were marching to burn the supply center at Danbury, Connecticut, he said, and the New York militia needed Sybil's father, Colonel Henry Ludington, to lead his company in defense.

Colonel Ludington was ready to serve, but there was a problem. His volunteer militiamen lived in lonely hamlets and on isolated farms scattered throughout the countryside. Someone would have to make the forty-mile ride to summon them to the mill. The rider who brought the news of the enemy raid was too exhausted to spread the alarm, and Colonel Ludington was needed at the mill to muster in the volunteers, examine their weapons and prepare them for the march.

Sybil offered a solution. "I'll go," she said. Colonel Ludington thought about the outlaws, deserters and robbers who plundered the district, and he decided the ride was not safe for a young girl. But Sybil pointed out that she knew the country well and that the volunteers knew her. Colonel Ludington finally gave his consent.

Sybil mounted Star, her father's horse, and took off into the night on her daring journey. Only rough trails and narrow, unmarked ox-cart roads led to many of the volunteers' homes, and the most densely populated areas were little more than crossroads. But Sybil galloped through the darkness, stopping before country taverns and lonely cabins long enough to pound on each door with a stick and shout, "The British are burning Danbury! Come right away!"

It was dawn when Sybil returned from her heroic ride. Already about a dozen of her father's militiamen were gathered on the drill ground behind the mill, and she could see more arriving. Exhausted and shivering from the cold spring air, Sybil climbed off of Star and into a warm bed.

The volunteers who responded to Sybil's cry that night intercepted the British troops in time to help drive them back to their ships in Long Island Sound. Sybil continues to be remembered today as "the female Paul Revere."

Sybil Ludington

SUSAN LIVINGSTON

Susan Livingston was the eldest of three daughters of William Livingston, the first elected governor of New Jersey. She and her sisters were so beautiful that they were known as the Three Graces. They were also very proud of their father, who was an important figure in the Americans' fight for independence. The British had attempted to capture him many times, but he decided to remain anyway at the family home.

A British soldier demands to search Susan Livingston's home.

In February 1779, Governor Livingston learned that British troops had landed at Elizabethtown Point, intending to take him prisoner. He made a quick escape, knowing that his wife and daughters could remain safely behind. When the British arrived at the Livingston home, they were disappointed to find the governor gone, but they were determined to find any war secrets among the papers he left behind.

Susan, her mother and sisters knew they could not defend their father's library from the soldiers, so they waited in a room upstairs. But Susan became so curious about the activity outside that she stepped boldly out onto a veranda roof to see the mounted redcoats below. A British officer saw her, rode up and politely instructed her to return inside for her own safety. Susan turned to go in, then discovered that the window had slammed shut and she could not reopen it. The officer, seeing her difficulty, dismounted, climbed to the veranda roof, forced the window open and helped her inside.

Susan smiled prettily, thanked him and asked his name. "Lord Cathcart," he said. Then, to his surprise, she offered to take him to the library where he could examine her father's papers at his ease. In return, she said, she asked only that he respect a lady's privacy and refrain from reading her personal letters that she kept in a carriage bag in the parlor. The gentlemanly Lord Cathcart agreed not to disturb the bag, and he even assigned a soldier to guard it during the house search. Susan then showed him the library and left him to read the governor's papers. He found only old legal documents and nothing of value to the British.

As Lord Cathcart rode away that day, he did not guess that in the carefully guarded carriage bag in the parlor was Governor Livingston's correspondence with the Congress, state officials and with General Washington.

Susan Livingston

GRACE and RACHEL MARTIN

Grace and Rachel Martin were living with their mother-in-law near Fort Ninety-Six, a British outpost in South Carolina, while their husbands were off fighting the redcoats. One day, Grace and Rachel learned that a British courier, carrying important dispatches to another British fort, was to pass that night along the road. The women hatched a scheme. Their plan was to hold up the British courier on his way to Fort Ninety-Six, take his dispatches and send them to an American camp.

Rachel Martin dressed in her husband's clothing and armed with a flintlock long rifle.

The two girls dressed in their husbands' clothing and carried their rifles a short way down the road where they knew the courier must pass. There they hid behind a rail fence and some bushes until dusk. When the British courier and his two escorts appeared on horseback, Grace and Rachel sprang out and pointed their rifles at the three men.

In deep, disguised voices, they ordered the soldiers to halt and raise their hands. Though the men had rifles of their own, they were so taken by surprise that they instantly surrendered. The girls then demanded the courier's papers, and he handed them over. Since they now had what they wanted, Grace and Rachel told the soldiers they were free to go.

The two then hurried home through a shortcut in the woods and immediately delivered the dispatches to a trusted messenger, who carried them to the nearest American camp.

The three flustered British soldiers, meanwhile, decided that there was nothing to do but start their journey back to Fort Ninety-Six in the morning. They rode back to a house they had passed earlier, hoping to get lodging for the night.

The elder Mrs. Martin, Grace and Rachel's mother-in-law, answered their knock at the door. The woman innocently asked if she had not seen them going by in the opposite direction a short time earlier. Embarrassed, they explained that they had been held up by two rebel lads armed with rifles.

Mrs. Martin agreed to put up the British soldiers overnight. The next morning they met and talked politely with Grace and Rachel, never imagining that they were sharing breakfast with the "rebel lads" who had held them up the previous night.

Grace and Rachel Martin

MARY LINDLEY MURRAY

In September 1776, British General William Howe's troops were in quick pursuit of the Continental army in New York. Washington divided his command into three parts for the retreat. Two of the three armies quickly escaped north, but the third army, led by General Israel Putnam, was laden with stores and ammunition and moved more slowly.

As General Putnam's soldiers plodded north beside the Hudson River, Howe's 8,000 men were less than a mile to the east. Thinking he had the rebels in an easy trap at the southern tip of Manhattan Island, Howe ordered his tired and hungry troops to rest. They stopped at Murray Hill, about halfway up Manhattan Island.

Murray Hill was named for Robert Murray, a wealthy New York merchant who had a country home there. Robert was a loyal supporter of England, but his wife Mary and their two daughters were staunch American patriots.

Mary knew that Howe needed only to continue his march west to cut off General Putnam's retreat, so she devised a plan. She sent a servant to General Howe with an invitation to visit her home. The general knew Mr. Murray was a true-blue loyalist, and he gladly accepted.

Many American solidiers owed their lives to the cunning of Mary Murray.

For two hours or more, the British general and his officers sat in the spacious parlor of the Murray mansion, happily talking, drinking homemade wine and brandies, and eating homemade cakes. Each time the general suggested it was time to leave, Mary found a way to stall the officers into prolonging their visit. She was determined to buy time for General Putnam, marching his troops a short distance to the west to join the rest of the American army at the northern tip of Manhattan.

Finally, Mary used her last idea for keeping the British officers entertained. She asked her serving maid to sing a song brought over from London. The officers sat through seven stanzas of "Sally in Our Alley" as the Continentals slipped safely from Howe's grasp.

After the Revolution, when a tablet commemorating Mary was unveiled, speaker George McVay said, "It was ever afterward the remark of the American army that during the darkest period in the history of the Revolutionary War it was saved, and our present independence secured, through Robert Murray's wine and the wit of his wife, Mary Lindley Murray."

Mary Lindley Murray

MOLLY PITCHER
(Mary Ludwig Hays)

In spite of British shot and shell, brave Mary Hays (Molly Pitcher) carried water from a stream to thirsty American soldiers at the battle of Monmouth, New Jersey.

Molly Hays was accompanying her husband's regiment, the Pennsylvania artillery, on the scorching hot Sunday in June 1778 when the Americans faced General Henry Clinton's redcoats at the battle of Monmouth, New Jersey. The heat was so intense that day that many of the soldiers collapsed as they fought, and their cries for "Water!" rang out across the battlefield.

Molly quickly grabbed an old stone pitcher with a broken spout. Disregarding the British fire all around her, she hurried back and forth from a nearby stream, delivering water to the parched soldiers. They soon learned the name of the brave woman with the precious water, and before long, their cries turned from "Water! Over here, Molly!" to "Molly! Pitcher!" This is how Mary Ludwig Hays became known as "Molly Pitcher."

When Molly wasn't carrying her pitcher from soldier to soldier that day, she was rescuing and nursing wounded men. She even lifted one disabled soldier onto her strong shoulders and carried him to the rear of the battle for medical treatment.

But perhaps the most astounding feat Molly accomplished that sweltering day was for her husband, John. As a gunner, John was assigned to swab out his cannon with a wet sponge, and then fire at the enemy. When Molly saw him hit by a British shell, she helped men carry him out of the line of fire to wait for the field surgeon's attention.

Then, at John's request, she returned to the unattended cannon. With no gunner to serve it, the crew was about to drag the gun away. "Don't take it away!" Molly told them. "I can take care of it." She fired the cannon under the blazing sun until the end of the battle. Her face became grimy with powder, smoke and dust, and her strong arms ached with the hard work.

When the fighting finally stopped, Molly went to the rear and, finding that John was not seriously injured, returned to the battlefield to carry more water and tend to wounded soldiers.

Word of Molly's heroics spread among the soldiers and reached General Washington. The next morning, the American commander personally thanked her and made her a sergeant.

Molly Pitcher

ESTHER DE BERDT REED
and
SARAH FRANKLIN BACHE

Some patriot women donated their jewelry and other valuables to be exchanged for cash to support the cause of liberty.

Though born in England, Esther de Berdt Reed was as strong an American patriot as anybody. Married to the governor of Pennsylvania and the mother of six young children, she organized a group of Philadelphia women to collect donations for George Washington's soldiers. The women solicited door-to-door in Philadelphia, Germantown, rural Pennsylvania and New Jersey, asking even the servants for donations. Some citizens sold their jewelry so that they would have cash to donate to the women.

The volunteers collected more than $7,500--a large sum then. In a letter to General Washinton, Esther suggested that the money be given directly to the soldiers as a reward for their service, but the commander wanted the donations to be used to provide shirts for the men instead. Esther then organized a committee of thirty-nine women to cut and sew shirts for the ragged army. But less than two weeks after the sewing project had begun, Esther died of dysentery.

Another young Philadelphia wife and mother, Sarah Franklin Bache, took over the project. Sarah, who was the daughter of Benjamin Franklin, continued to raise funds and roused great public interest in the project from men as well as women. Soon Sarah had a corps of Pennsylvania women helping her to cut out and manufacture shirts.

In January 1780, General Washington gratefully accepted 2,200 shirts for his army. The winter was a bitter one, and the shirts made by the women of Philadelphia helped hundreds of soldiers in Washington's camp to survive.

The general wrote to Sarah, "I pray you now to be persuaded, that a sense of the patriotic exertions of yourself and the ladies who have furnished so handsome and useful a gratuity for the army, at so critical and severe a season, will not easily be effaced, and that the value of the donation will be greatly enhanced by a consideration of the hands by which it was made and presented."

Mrs. Reed and Mrs. Bache

MARY SLOCUMB

Mary Slocumb spent that entire Monday in February 1776 worrying about her husband, Lieutenant Ezekiel Slocumb. Zeke and his company of eighty soldiers had marched off the day before to battle a company of loyalists on their way to join the British army. Mary and her small child stayed behind at the couple's plantation in Wayne County, North Carolina.

That night, Mary had a horrible nightmare. She dreamed that a bloody corpse, surrounded by dead and wounded soldiers, lay wrapped in her husband's military cloak. Mary awoke with a start. "I must go to him!" she cried. She instructed a servant to look after her child, and set off with her mare in a mad gallop down the road.

Mary didn't know where to find Zeke, so she followed the road the men had taken nearly two days before. By dawn she was thirty miles from home and saw no sign of Zeke's soldiers. In another few hours, however, she could hear the roar of cannon and the crackle of rifle fire. She rode toward the thunder until she came upon the battle of Moore's Creek Bridge and the scene of her nightmare. About twenty men lay under some trees. One of them was wrapped in her husband's cloak, just as she had seen in her dream.

Mary Slocumb bids farewell to her husband as he marches off to battle.

Horrorstruck, Mary jumped from her horse and raced to the body. She uncovered the head and found a face bathed in blood and gore. The man was alive. He weakly begged for water; Mary didn't recognize the voice. She found a kettle and carried water from a nearby stream. When she wiped away the blood, she discovered that the wounded man was a neighbor. His leg hurt more than his head, he told her, so Mary cut away his trousers, and found that a bullet had ripped a hole through his calf. Because she had no bandages, Mary pressed a handful of large leaves against the wound to stop the bleeding. She then turned her attention to the other wounded men, and she cared for them all day and far into the night.

Mary was overjoyed when her husband rode up. Although he was covered with mud and blood, he was unharmed and amazed to see her there. He wanted her to ride back to the plantation the next day with a guard of troops, but Mary was anxious to return to their child. She left alone in the middle of the night. When she arrived safely at home, she had covered 125 miles on horseback and gone forty hours without sleep.

Mary Slocumb

JANE THOMAS

Jane Thomas and her husband, Colonel John Thomas, lived in South Carolina with their nine children during the height of the Revolutionary struggle there. Though Jane was proud when her husband and their sons joined the fight against the British, she was heartsick when John and two of her boys were taken prisoner. The Thomases were confined at Fort Ninety-Six, a British-held outpost in western South Carolina.

Despite her advanced age, Jane one day rode her horse the long distance from her home in the Spartanburg District to visit her husband and sons in captivity. While she was there, she happened to overhear a group of Tory women discuss the war. "Tomorrow night the loyalists intend to surprise the rebels at Cedar Spring," one of the women told the others.

Jane's heart raced when she heard these words. Cedar Springs was only a few miles from her home, and her second eldest son was part of a garrison of about sixty American soldiers encamped there. Jane knew that if Cedar Springs was captured, the Tories would kill or imprison the American soldiers there and then pillage the area for miles around.

Jane was at least fifty miles from Cedar Springs when she overheard the alarming news, and she was already tired from the day's travel. But she knew she must get to Cedar Springs as quickly as possible to warn the Americans, so she mounted her horse and pushed it to a gallop. She hurried along rough trails, through woods and swamps and across two rivers. Though Jane grew more weak from hunger and fatigue as each hour passed, she urged her weary horse on.

When she finally reached her son's camp, Jane delivered the warning. The grateful soldiers immediately made a plan. They would leave their campfires burning bright but take their rifles into the darkness of the surrounding woods to await the Tories. Jane, meanwhile, turned for home. She was near exhaustion, but at least she and her tired horse could travel the route home more slowly.

Later Jane learned that when the Tories arrived at Cedar Springs that night, they rushed the camp for their surprise attack. But it was they rather than the Americans who were surprised. Only a few loyalists escaped the ambush; the rest were taken prisoner by Jane's son and the other patriots.

An exhausted Jane Thomas rides home after warning the American soldiers encamped at Cedar Springs about the planned Tory attack.

Jane Thomas

SALLY TOWNSEND

The American forces were always kept informed of British activities by many young patriot heroines.

Sally Townsend was a teen-aged girl who lived on Long Island in New York. She kept her patriotism to herself, because several British officers were staying in the Townsend home.

Sally was cooking alone in the kitchen one day when a neighbor snuck in through the back door. He did not see Sally, who stood motionless in the corner. The man put a paper in the cupboard, then quickly left. Sally waited a few seconds, then rushed to the cupboard. The paper appeared to be a routine business letter addressed to someone named John Anderson. It mentioned West Point, a patriot fortress fifty miles away. Sally didn't understand what the message meant, but she knew the British wanted to control West Point and the Hudson River. She secretly watched the kitchen, and before long, John André, a British major who sometimes visited the house, quietly slipped in to retrieve the message.

Later that day, Sally overheard West Point mentioned in a conversation between Major André and a British colonel. She decided to relate the suspicious activity to her older brother, who managed their father's store in New York City and who also worked as a patriot spy. Sally sent her brother a carefully worded message with a request for a package of tea.

When the messenger returned with the tea, Sally found a note inside. Her brother told her to contact some men on Long Island's North Shore. The men in turn relayed the information to a patriot boatman. The boatman crossed the Sound, and awaited a secret signal. When he saw a black petticoat hanging on a line beside three white handkerchiefs, he delivered the message to a patriot spy on shore. The spy then forwarded the message to Major Benjamin Tallmadge.

Major Tallmadge was interested in the message, because he had earlier received a note from General Benedict Arnold requesting an escort for a Mr. John Anderson. When a pair of militiamen found Anderson wandering behind the American lines, Tallmadge ordered that he be brought in for questioning. The patriots then discovered that John Anderson was really Major André, and papers found inside his boot connected Benedict Arnold in a traitorous scheme with the British. Sally's shrewd eyes and quick action had helped uncover Benedict Arnold's plan to betray his country and turn West Point over to the British.

Sally Townsend

MERCY OTIS WARREN

Many American women shared Mercy Otis Warren's love of liberty.

On their farm in Plymouth, Massachusetts, Mercy Otis Warren and her husband, James, sat in front of the fireplace with company. The year was 1765, and Mercy's father and brother had come for a visit from Boston. They brought the latest news from the colony's capital, where Mercy's brother James was a member of the Massachusetts Assembly.

James Otis talked about the Stamp Act, which had recently been passed by the British Parliament. It required colonists to purchase stamps for many items, including all legal and commercial papers. Mercy felt angry that Britain had suddenly decided to levy a tax upon the colonists. She believed in self-government and that the colonies' representative assemblies should be responsible for taxing the colonists.

James Warren had an idea. He knew that his wife was always writing letters and discussing colonial problems, usually more effectively than the Boston newspaper writers. "Why don't you write some letters about this?" he suggested. "We could make copies and pass them around. They may open many eyes to what is going on."

Mercy was the mother of five sons and had little time for such a project. But in spite of her home and farm duties, Mercy made time to write and denounce Britain's new taxation policy and other parliamentary measures limiting the colonies' authority. "And be it known to Britain," Mercy wrote, "even American daughters are politicians and patriots, and will aid the good work with their female efforts."

Mercy was a skillful writer with a gift for persuasion. Before long she became one of the best-known writers in Massachusetts. Her pamphlets were widely distributed, and her anti-British poems and articles were published in newspapers and journals. She also penned several plays ridiculing England, though not under her own name, since it was considered improper for women to write satire.

Thanks to the political writings of Mercy and her friend, Abigail Adams, anti-British sentiment grew in the colonies. After independence had been won, Mercy made a final contribution to her country with her *History of the Rise, Progress, and Termination of the American Revolution.*

"...American daughters are politicians and patriots, and will aid the good work ..." - Mercy Otis Warren

MARGARET TODD WHETTEN

Times were hard for Margaret Whetten in Manhattan. British soldiers had seized New York, and Margaret was a staunch patriot. Then, when her sick husband died, Margaret was left to raise the children alone. Her only money was Continental paper, which was practically worthless. It took careful planning to feed the family on so little money, but nearly every day Margaret and her daughters took or sent food and clothes to American soldiers held prisoner by the British in the city jails. At one prison, the jailer let them sit at the window and talk to the prisoners who were nearly starving in the yard below. Margaret also frequently made mush from Indian meal for American soldiers in hospitals and sent provisions to inmates on prison ships.

On more than one occasion, Margaret risked her own safety by opening her home to people suspected of aiding the American cause. One day she learned that British soldiers were coming to her home to arrest one of her patriot guests. Margaret quickly grabbed a dressing gown and nightcap and instructed the man to put it on. When the British soldiers arrived, they found their intended prisoner in bed clothes, seated in a big easy chair and weakly eating from a bowl of soup. Margaret told the soldiers that the man was too sick to be taken away, and she persuaded them to return after she had nursed him back to health. When the British commanding officer learned that the soldiers had allowed the suspect to remain free, he ordered them to return at once and arrest the man. Back at the Whetton house, the soldiers discovered that the "invalid" was gone.

Now Margaret came under suspicion of harboring and protecting American spies, so the British officer posted a guard across the street to watch the Whetten house. Margaret welcomed the attention because it discouraged intruders. However, she hated having to host thirsty British officers who stopped in frequently for punch. They sometimes flung their empty glasses to the ceiling, shattering them into a thousand pieces. Other redcoats were more polite but wary, and they referred to her home as "Rebel Headquarters."

After the war, General Washington came to breakfast with Margaret, and personally thanked her for her efforts.

Margaret Todd Whetten and her daughters bring food to American prisoners held in British jails in occupied New York.

Margaret Todd Whetten

ELIZABETH ZANE

Betty Zane and her two brothers lived in a small frontier settlement known as Fort Henry, Virginia. The older brother, Colonel Ebenezer Zane, lived in a cabin that was well fortified and contained a storage place for gunpowder. Betty and her brother Silas lived inside the fort with about sixty other men, women and children.

One September day in 1782, nearly 350 Indians and British soldiers attacked the fort. They gave the settlers two options: surrender or be massacred. "Never!" the settlers shouted, and a long series of assaults began.

Soon the supply of gunpowder ran low in the fort. Ebenezer's cabin was only sixty yards away. To get to the cabin and gunpowder would mean crossing through a hail of gunfire. All eighteen of the men volunteered for the dangerous duty, but Betty was determined to try. "I can run as fast as any man, and you have no man to spare," she told Silas and Ebenezer. Besides, she argued, she knew where the gunpowder was stored and would have a better chance at reaching the cabin since the enemy would never suspect a girl of such a mission.

So Betty slowly strolled outside of the gate as if she were on an afternoon walk. The Indians and redcoats were so amazed and curious to see Betty that she reached her destination before they fired a shot.

Inside the cabin, Betty snatched the cloth off a table, poured a keg of powder into it, and folded the corners to make a bag. She knew that returning to the fort would not be so easy. This time the Indians and redcoats would be ready to fire on her, and she must run for the fort. She took off her long skirt and petticoats so she wouldn't be slowed down, and then she bounded from the cabin with the gunpowder slung over her shoulder.

Sharpshooters in the fort tried to distract the enemy, but bullets flew all around Betty as she raced for the fort. Once she stumbled, but she picked herself up in a hurry and ran on. When she reached the fort, the men inside opened the gate at the last possible moment, and Betty darted inside with the precious bag of gunpowder. A huge cheer rose up from the men and women.

Though the siege would last another day and night, the settlers did not run out of gunpowder, and the attackers eventually gave up and fled.

Elizabeth Zane

FAITH ROBINSON TRUMBULL

American women made donations of clothing and valuables to help the ragged, starving Continental soldiers at Valley Forge, Penna.

The winter of 1777-78 was bleak for the Continental Army. Thousands of soldiers encamped at Valley Forge were hungry, cold, sick and dying. Throughout the colonies, churches regularly collected contibutions of money, groceries and even bullets after Sunday services to benefit the suffering men.

In Connecticut, Governor Jonathan Trumbull was in charge of organizing and collecting the donations, but it was his wife, Faith Robinson Trumbull, who is remembered as the inspiring fund raiser.

One Sunday morning after a service in Lebanon, Connecticut, the minister called for donations for the troops. Without hesitating, Faith arose from her seat beside her husband, removed a magnificent red cloak from her shoulders and carried it to the front of the church as her contibution for the Continental Army. The pastor recalled later that the gesture "so aroused the enthusiasm of the congregation that a large donation was made." Men and women followed Faith to the altar with gifts of rings, gold chains, purses, caps, scarves, money, clothing and written promises of provisions.

Faith's beautiful cloak, which had been a gift from the French commander Comte de Rochambeau, was eventually cut into strips and used to trim American soldiers' uniforms.

For more, ***The Story of Our Flag*** will enthrall you!